Watershed

Watershed

new Finger Lakes poems

by

Carolyn Clark

Cover design by Shay Culligan
Cover image by Daphne Solá
Author's photo by Katherine Solomon

ISBN: 978-1-63980-296-8

Kelsay Books
502 South 1040 East, A-119
American Fork, Utah 84003
Kelsaybooks.com

Preface

Our watershed moments are not always huge, as on the Continental Divide, but rather, as so many things in nature, minute, in miniature, whether numerous or few. Drops of rain or porticos of snow always become a source of life, the very same that will suage our thirst.

Start with where you live—do you know what watershed you are in?

I'd like to thank all my family, friends, and readers new and old, for inspiring this book. I am especially grateful to my husband Geoff for "following the river" together—and for insisting on our latest project: the rain barrel.

Many of these new poems, some having been resuscitated, were written to share with my friends at OPG (Our Poetry Group), in meetings (in person or in hybrid Zoom) every six weeks for four+ years, including during the Covid-19 pandemic.

I am doubly thankful to my editor and publisher Karen Kelsay for bringing yet another of my poetry manuscripts to life, one in 2019 and now this one in 2023, from trees to human hands. We poets can be as intractable as bees, especially me—or in my case, my antique typewriter QWERTY—already on the move to write "the next one."

To paraphrase Homer, *the newest song is like the dawn, what pleases the most.*
Odyssey 1.351–352

τὴν γὰρ ἀοιδὴν μᾶλλον ἐπικλείουσ᾽ ἄνθρωποι,
ἥ τις ἀκουόντεσσι νεωτάτη ἀμφιπέληται.

In Homer's *Odyssey,* upon hearing the bard starts singing anew of the battles at Troy, Penelope weeps, asking him to steer away from the topic. Her son Telemachus strongly objects, arguing that 'men praise that song the most *which comes the newest to their ears* (1.351–2) (Gregory Nagy translation).

Today it is climate change that is now the constant, long battleground in our lives. In *Watershed,* we are invited to read and listen, and maybe even transform our ways.

Acknowledgments

The Avocet: A Journal of Nature Poems: "Artemis Dream—Opening Day of Hunting Season"

Bluff & Vine Literary Review, Issue Five (2021): "Manure Pile Muse," "Ever Green," "Christmas Miracle: Nativity Scene in Virgil, NY"

Cold War Vol. 1: The Cold War—Living Under Its Shadow: "Wintergarden Cold War *Redux*" (the dedication poem)

Ekphrastic Review Writing Challenge: "Dead Bells of Ireland"

From the Finger Lakes: a Memoir Anthology: "*Lares* Love Poem #2," "COVID-19 *Lares* Love Poem #6"

Plainsongs 42.2: "Untact"

Poem in Your Pocket Series, Tompkins County Public Library: "Ocean Blues Yellow," "*Spes* (Hope) is all around," "Two Shooting Stars"

Red Wolf Editions, Journeying (Fall 2020): "Arrival CDG—2014"

Sibyl Journal: "Untitled," a QWERTY poem—for Mom/Florence A. Clark

Society of Classical Poets: "The River"

When the Virus Came Calling: COVID-19 Strikes America: "Windowsill Prayer: A Precursor to COVID-19," "To the Mask Makers," "*Lares* Love Poem #2," "COVID-19 *Lares* Love Poem #6"

Contents

Arrival CDG—2014

for Sean and Caroline

Our white mare follows me
even across oceans:
transported inadvertently
past *la douane*
one white horsehair
on my jacket, brand "Avalanche."

This level crossing of *la banlieue*
the Blue line at first glance so similar to Rockville's
Red line: above ground, green and below . . .

but—Sycamores—here there are more of them,
Isis' gift,
and ubiquitous graffiti.

Similarities abound,
parallels to Tribeca, trains of NY.

Yet here these trees adapt, hang on.
And graffiti? Why try to erase
that which cannot be (erased).
A deeper history here relives the pain
of centuries as if it were yesterday, or
tomorrow.

I'm crossing towards Paris past
crumbled buildings and crumpled litter
that still swirls in place,

yet today the early light,
and hope, slices of fresh shade,
cool in summer,
put on a fresh face.

Amish-Built Carport

for Joseph

July 17, 2018

Newfield, NY

Carpe Carportem
here's a post mortem
you're built—now what?

Trees to lumber connected
still can story tell:
in arms and roots well-placed.
holding 2:1 Clear to Redwood stain,
in lodgepole pine stature,
Thai-picturesque portal, lean-to
arms upholding snow and rain
for future seasons, the same
green metal roof as over
~ our home ~
the one hewn by hand,
yours, and with God's help,
it came together.

The winds will test you, *Carportem,*
lightening dance reflections in you—
thunderclaps resound off you—

yet may the days and nights
that oaken your coat
keep us all Hail-free,
o delicate umbrella,
        comrade,
beneath this shared Heaven.

Artemis Dream—Opening Day of Hunting Season

Shotgun shot
wakes me from a dream
so suddenly that
I lose it,
trailing off, into light
so blonde it must be dawn.

Opening Day of Hunting Season.

In a flash I invoke *Potnia Theron*
(Queen of Wild Animals, once the mighty
Ishtar—Nana on Lion—Aphrodite).
Sole Artemis, guardian of deer.
After her demise, her roles fragmented
into a down-sized figurine: archer or bather
by woodland pools where water runs swift as wind.

Goddess of the chase and chastity,
and yet somehow she knows
birth pangs, the pain of another's labor.

Her preferences? Solitary company,
or perhaps a small circle of young girls.

Hasten, shadows, ferns and gullies.
No Tinker Bell she:
heliotropic
in the forest canopy, gleaning
sunshine wherever it falls, filters.

One loud shot, then another, buckshot,
followed by footfalls (each shoe
a *cauda* (tail) repeating itself,

as if a coda, colon or semicolon)
in the woods of our neighboring gorge.

Who would dare go there today?
Even our black dog stays close,
points, sniffs around the woodpile,
smells death and smoke wafting up from the gulf
while I linger inside, sipping coffee
till these gunshots at last subside, fade off
to the shuffle of my moccasin slippers.

But I promise myself
at night to look up her lovers—

disloyal Orion, or those who espied,
like Actaeon,
all whose stories are written in the stars,

while all the while
Artemis keeps on trying
to protect her wild animals,
desires only

to keep them wild,
wild and far away—
procul harum—
far from these things.

Briar Patch *Caveat*

Reckless thicket,
fit as a fiddle
but wide in the middle,
time has tricked you
once again: you are
no longer nine!

Surrounded by knotty pine,
a crisscross of logs
sustains you—almost
a senior citizen—
with more time and less energy
to get things done: *agenda*
is a to-do list.

Today's Inbox addictive,
yesterday's accomplishments
all old hat now.

Local travel of briars,
frequent flyers christening the sky,
birds escaping a tangerine cat
to the blue eggshell heaven
so fragile in its free-range yolk,
your crimson dot, like Covid's,
dictates the purple spring
will soon begin, and 2020,
nay, now 2021 and 2022
comes with a caveat:

grandchildren, go 'round!

Manure Pile Muse

Two false cognates
—*burgeon* and *bourgeois*—
spring to mind
as each fewer manure pile
multiplies with flies.
I shovel gingerly,
grateful my back is now
bending in ways
that didn't work last spring.

We've come all the way,
from manic May
to quirky October.
The first frost is late,
yet leaves are somehow bright,
no thanks to climate change
in this our region—Finger Lakes (FLX).
More people are moving here,
some coming back
from Los Angeles (LAX)
to our lush, green Arcadia—Newfield, NY.

Like manure-pile flies,
we *burgeon* as the new *bourgeoisie,*
cell phones in hand, even me—
musing through the morning chores
making less room for more,
just one stop away from extinction.

bur·geon /ˈbərjən/
verb
gerund or present participle: **burgeoning**
begin to grow or increase rapidly; flourish.
"manufacturers are keen to cash in on the burgeoning demand"

archaic•literary
put forth young shoots; bud.
Origin: Middle English: from Old French *bourgeonner* 'put out buds,' from *borjon* 'bud,' based on late Latin *burra* 'wool.'

bour·geois /ˈboorZHwä/
adjective
adjective: **bourgeois**
1.   of or characteristic of the middle class, typically with reference to its
     perceived materialistic values or conventional attitudes.
"a rich, bored, bourgeois family"
mid-16th century: from French, from late Latin *burgus* 'castle' (in medieval Latin 'fortified town'), ultimately of Germanic origin and related to *borough*. Cf. *burgess*.

Christmas Miracle: Nativity Scene in Virgil, NY

The boys' and girls' entrances on the closed school,
goats and sheep perched on snowbanks
in the side yard of an old white house by the fire department sign
a Shetland pony stands at the door
at 6 degrees Fahrenheit
the wind drifting the snow from the public graveyard
onto a road that winds before time
like a magic carpet leading to the nearby resort
a mist is thick with snowmaking,
trees glistening gray and golden
as a Bruegel landscape.

Death and Taxes Eve

Riding again
got my permit today
reported back to the barn
from the WSSC watershed.

The winds are at it again
but no new trees down
just the usual crisscross
rough and tumble
log cabin style
old cedars
down
and
out-
right
decay,
decadent
rusting red
organ donors
doing their job
better than me—
and so very soon
they'll all be covered
with green laurel and holly shrubs
so much so
that I won't be able to cut through—
and there'll be lots more spider webs too . . .

Eire I: A Sketch of Sleigh Head

Lime cliffs and TB calves
the creamery
the bathtub
honeycomb
tombs and hedges
heretic monks
high cliffs
a rag lady—Dicey Riley—
root walking stick
drawn directions
by a gnarled old man
in Gaelic only: Kruger's
wolf sun
summer moon
rare flowers
coldest beaches
large stones
deep pebbles
prairie cliffs
off the Blasket Islands
the most western point
facing west—*Ryan's Daughter*
a movie-village razed
dubbed famous now.

Pain and poverty hand in hand
with music before Philomela
me,
trusting instinct to guide sure steps,
wordless,
a color only,
seeing glistening salmon rawboned
in the green river of my imagination

no prior knowledge of what I was
seeing
but *a priori* roots
sunk deep and tingled,
Jungian, genetic
as the orange
discus set
over Sleigh Head.

Elenchos

Ancient Greek—argument, dialogue, refutation, trial, test

Under midday sun
thought oozes,
emerging
from hefty cracks
of dry earth,
night frozen
in her nakedness.

Two men are left,
spines supported by
a wizened weather tree,
sheltering their heads
with fists and fingerlets
of curls: dusty silver leaves,
small damp olives
that shine like black stars at noon.

Elenchos, a first dialogue,
almost begins:
     a word is born softly alone
     and shuffles off to nothing.
     The other word emits a hollow "Oh"—
     leaves no echo.

Nothing but impossible red dust
settles over this dead harbor bathed in salt.
The men secrete saliva in trembling bubbles
that blister into spittle, useless to whet the wind.

They crave new breath—even *meltemi*—
to blow out the light, sift through the crystal
moisture of tired grass, and rescue them
from abandoned obscurity,

to secure,
once and for all,
their careless,
ceaseless
prayer.

Ever Green

for Mark

Each ornament
adorns
remembrances,
sparks recognition,
delights.

Concolor from Oregon seed
wintered here some eleven years,
according to its cut stump,
post-drought.

Laughing, we snap pics of our find:
Geoff with bowsaw in his teeth,
me leaning like an elf, again
in Mark's forest: *Fir Farm*

where the trees run free
above and below deep ruts
his tractor keeps tracking
back and forth, over the years

where bluebirds perch,
ragweed is queen
and the wild things *are . . .*
ever green.

Final Twist

When told
never look back
trust in the gods
believe in your beloved
Orpheus could not
follow orders
resist doubt,
longing, temptation,
sought her out
with his own eyes.

In the dusk he found
his beautiful Eurydice
just a footstep behind his,
following him
upstairs,
her shining face long
as if a kitchen match
held under her chin
a buttercup of infinity
wrestled from their field.

So as he glanced back
daring to meet
the adoring gaze
he knew was his
(and love comes in at the eye)
their eyes like lovers met,
etched in forever
that moment

she vanished.

Windowsill Prayer: A Precursor to COVID-19

for Stacey

April 3, 2020

Let me polish my grief
like stones from the creek
       lucky stones
pulled from time's passage
and brought home
to stay on the sill
quite well-oiled,
       still.

Let me feel the refrain
of repetition each day
in prayers and thoughts
that otherwise
       like birds
would fly away.

Let me feed them, my soul,
it's hard to survive,
to let yourself feel
and still be alive—
to shake the quilt of open spaces
of open spaces
that so few can have
while Covid-19 cuts
its wide swathe.

Let my sadness shine in tears,
       warm and salty.
       compassionate,
          real.

To the Mask Makers[*]

Bartels Hall

April 8, 2020

After using the handwashing station
and receiving a newly minted mask
and a Visitor tag
I am let in to see inside
Cornell's glossy basketball arena, center court,
where in just a handful of days
you have made a difference:
a make-shift factory,
where daily more well-coordinated volunteers jump
to make new light blue masks, strong ones,
for health workers, those near the frontlines,
for vulnerable populations, for senior citizens
including me—as asthma's my night visitor—
for all who soon will learn to wear masks,
people and children,
we all who now need masks.

For how long, we may ask?
For as long as plague-bearing
Apollo of the far-shooting arrows
binds us in his sight
his curved bow tight,
for as long as merciless Fates—
Clotho, Lachesis, and dread Atropos—
keep up their spin, apportion and cut us down
just to remind us of how fragile we humans are,
our bodies, if not our spirits, worn thin by pandemic,
just so long,
that's how long we'll need masks.

31

And for this your team wisdom, strength, foresight,
dedication and resolve,
I thank you, my friend, and all you volunteers, I thank you
for making this year, this 2020 and Covid-19 and
the unbearable lightness of being
somehow more bearable.

** Thank you, Cindy D., and all the volunteers who barely looked up from their
work, while I came to see and reap for myself this amazing spectacle.*

Lares Love Poem #2

for Sarah

April 10, 2020

Intrepid wind
you ignite my house
I cannot slow you down:
pollen or Amazon or both
you keep delivering more and more
than I ever asked for.

Like children our needs keep
changing: today the printer
tomorrow the pond pump
yesterday more *One-a-Days,*
vitamins to keep us strong.

Me? Sending masks and a thermometer
via USPS overnight to Brooklyn,
where the city that never sleeps
is now a sensory-deprivation box
and my youngest child's on fire
as a coal that keeps reigniting,
her jet-black hair unwinding
a coiled staircase over the courtyard
in my dreams: moist and dark,
Rapunzel's ladder,
the only way out.

Prayers also winging, though
taking flight, angels land on
breast and breath and shoulder
to give each statistic
strength, hope and human form.

COVID-19 *Lares* Love Poem #6

for OPG

April 16, 2020

Consolidate!
So now old projects can be done?
No interruptions, visitors, visits,
no destinations, so few appointments.
Write books, poetry, read and erase
imposed solitude of time and place.
Wear a mask, a persona,
but keeping one eye on heaven,
this Easter season feel no guilt
in rejoicing in nature,
more faith-filled than reason:

Look! From the window, over open field
the sleek fisher now streams away:
a dark, wave-like pulsing motion,
abandons stealth, leaps in slices from barn
to home to woods' edge.
This is no woodchuck lumbering
from old holes and rotten firewood
to dodge our axe.
No, it's a wild wave, a pulse in fresh snow,
dashing from where fox kits and fawns
flip night and day in play below
our neighboring, huge, iconic
broken-down barn-willow,
to race back and forth mown trails
to and fro to the frontlines: young poplars soon
bursting in leaf-song applause:
Stay! Stay! Stay the course!

Full Report at Eleven

*same day as "Breaking News: kayaker shot
by sharpshooter in Arundel Woods"*

Short shrift
half halt
the woods are full
of compound-sounding words:
duck blind
moonstruck
blood red
moonblind.

Anticipate
the full eclipse
of the full moon tonight . . .
a full report . . .

Obergurgl
undertone
kleine schrift—
we're not alone.

Tree frogs or peepers?
Who can distinguish
slate gray
from a great blue heron
still looming on the branch
overhanging this finger of an inlet?

I whisper into my mare's
furry soft white ear . . .
"Let's go Splish-Splash!"

Poetry is not on demand,
but if the creek is deep enough . . .
muddy fetlocks dance!

Nearby peepers hush,
a mallard pair rushes
out of nowhere, ambushing us,
their necks outstretched
like serpents hissing.

Half-Breath, Lighthearted

for Carol R. of OPG

Congestion isn't just about traffic.
Here's a short history: it's about shortness of breath.
This morning between thunderstorms
at digitally 3:00 a.m. my head lolls,
nostrils phlegm-filled, over-stuffed.
I've had *Enuff!*
No asthma (thankfully)
but a beachhead's rising
in my throat, enough to fill
three paper napkins.
It's no picnic, and then
when I re-enter our bed
my sweet hubby suggests,
why not go upstairs?
So here I lie,
propped up alone,
a first in so long,
measuring time to the tick
of clocks whose faces I cannot see.
Awake, despite a night's cocktail:
a tidbit of generic Benadryl,
Singular, in a half-warmed glass
of Bota-box white wine with lemon.
All this helps, as does sitting up
among old friends—
the books, toys, souvenirs and sachets
in this half-loft—my parents' old bed
still held together
by a single orange strap,
whose mattress can conform to my body
and won't squeak with my every
      half-breath.
I begin to feel grateful,

braced for dawn
like Athena's own pet owl,
able to look around and be glad
that the glass in hand,
and not my lungs,
is still half-full.

Happy Valentine's Day, Geoff!

Here's a pile of snowflakes
made from paper and scissors.

They are not hexagonal,
nor perfect, nor square,
but I made them for you—
like my heart—
so there!

Thank you for being my rock
(to paper and scissors).

I love you, more
than you'll ever know—
but stick around anyways.

Love,
unconditionally,

C.

Horse Sense Cowgirl

for a woman who has good HORSE SENSE
& brings about change in "an understated way"

Cowgirl clown guide
riding at our side,
lonesome together,
no threesome better:
Sharlene,
twig-snapping,
leaf-tossing laughter,
who's accomplished
more-horse-sense in one day,
helps me keep moving
this nervous elder mare
in the right direction,
gently, <<rester-Zen>>,
no reward needed ~
for a woman guide-rider
like that,
that cowgirl Sharlene.

In a nutshell: *hic et nunc*

Poesis and posies
so closely related:
best friends forever.

Mythos and *logos*
belittled, beleaguered
belong to a netherworld,
one I used to inhabit.

My passions rekindled
by a jello-legged little boy:
I have to be stronger
to lift him up, my spine opines,
skiing and falling, fast or slow,
out of control is still
one way to go.

Approaching the speed limit (65)
remember Wyoming—its wide open
spaces, where 85 is their norm
and winter's a bitch with jagged teats.

It's a dog's life: longer, shorter,
grateful for *em, vivo*
I am reconnoitering:
No Loitering.

Journaling in the Dark

Going through the motions until this fizzles out.
Winter and I are twinned, sibling, rival.
It reigns tonight: February the month of Fever.
Romans understood getting through this
was all that mattered.

In the meantime, honor thy Muse.
Foolish girl, if-you-can't-say-anything-nice,
don't-say-anything-at-all,
the winter wind rips into your heart
and takes a bite away

but you will stay until the appointed time lets you go:
until you are dismissed (class dismissed),
a substitute teacher, all washed up.

"—ing" things are all I've known—but for now,
walk slow. This change of course, a mid-winter rain,
derailment in the middle of the night—
a wind shear that grounds even the best planes,
horses, ski instructors . . . and all the "—er" things:
teacher, personal trainer, rider on the storm,
swimmer, runner, horse lover, driver,
now transform to just one goal—survivor.

I stay on, journaling in the dark,
not looking back, except to say, been-there,
done-that, was-that-so-bad?

It's not my voice that rattles in the night,
just the teeth we've lost.

Lares[*] Love Poem #1

for Geoff

April 3, 2020

Hi Ho Hi Ho it's off to work we go
Another day, another acronym.
So hard for our millennial kids to believe
that for a split second I actually thought
WFH means *What the F . . . Happened?*

LOL—Mom!—Did you really?
I feel like that for the first two seconds
of almost every morning I wake up.

But it's true. I did. I made up a new meaning.
Working from home? Maybe nothing new
but for a few it can still be
hell on earth.
You'd better like your roommate(s)!
<u>The Morning Brew</u> of my phone
announces today.

I thank my stars, and looking skyward,
flash 'em back a wonderful, *Yes!*
(like the one I said before I said *I do*—
and he did too).
How lucky that I get along with mine.
Aw, Geoff—say it like a sneeze!—
into an elbow or kerchief, please.

He often wears a prickly, three-day goatee,
a sign of the times, though soon to cycle through:
newly clean-shaven, his chin

is now smooth
as a baby's you-know-what,
and bright as the buttercup
I hold beneath.

* *Lares—Roman gods protecting the home, often a youthful pair of dancing statuettes;* figs. 2, 11 in *Tibullus Illustrated: Lares, Genius and Sacred Landscapes* (JHU diss.,1997) on ProQuest/Open View
https://www.proquest.com/openview/d802e5ca0ae4059f0fc84ada7155efe7/1?pq-origsite=gscholar&cbl=18750&diss=y

I Heart Solitude

Not to be rude, but day after day goes by
and I don't even fly. Why? Why?
Basil, mint and teas spend my garden knees.
The poet in me? Complacent. Or I work, editing:
ancient dog's eyes eking out cash from the screen,
sowing seeds of incremental blindness.
I keep spitting out sputum
as if life's pogroms may yet be found
in the heart's tall basement. Write where? on what?
Marble? Bronze? How about papyrus' cousin: paper.
Tonight a lost book, Marina Tsvetayeva's *Selected Poems,*
so long misplaced, is found!
Its slender frame still upright, and not much must.
Its pink and brown jacket charms: icon-like, she watches me
do prescribed stretches on my rust yoga matt.
She urges me: hurry up, get on with It!
Her left hand curled in a gentle fist,
forms a gentle sign, an O, a Q, almost a thumbs-up,
upholding her chin, a Thinker's pose, bemused.
Inside the book, inscribed, a heartfelt *Bon courage*
penned by a fellow poetry-lover, from Paros in '70-something:
"We have pens—we shall write!"

45

Marriage Paean

on a Labor Day Weekend

Only the simple things in life are true.
A man lives by intuition as long as he can,
building a deliberate life,
rocks and dreams counterpoised,
finds balance, and then a wife.

A woman raised on children's books
looks for beauty, tender looks, strength and shelter,
a soft-hearted man who can bring out the best
in herself, give her freedom, win her trust.

This day and age redefine our roles
but the longings remain the same:
live first for love, sweet harmony,
all else will fall in place.

Entering school again, with eyes that will not close
to worldly discomposure, ambition and the rose,
I feel a need for nurturing, for plants and things that grow,
you come to me more real than in a dream,

how could I let you go?

Shadow Odes: To a Strawberry

I.

Its constellations of seeds
uniform as pincushion
calico, with snippets doll-like
plump and long as rabbit ears
(my favorite object in my mother's sewing kit,
the multi-tiered one she'd take to sewing bees).
Taste this wild one—
the smallest have the most flavor—
the one I choose now,
from a small plate
of fresh fruits for the palate,
our local Poet Laureate leading us
where we workshop together,
tucked in a library room
to learn to write
poems about food.
I grind it slowly, savoring
seeds and all,
despite a recent bout
with diverticulitis,
my hand cannot resist
popping its juicy heart into my own
ruby red throat.

II.

Two years ago was the last spring I was
to offer wild strawberries
to my best friend's younger brother, A.,
destined to leave us too soon . . . what started
as "difficulty swallowing" blazed through him
an unmarked trail.
He was with us as guide and guard
for five starry nights, dewy mornings
while we three teens followed the Finger Lakes Trail
from Watkins Glen to Upper Buttermilk,
together making memories
of cooking up
wild strawberry pancakes in a boundless field . . .
where a shy, quiet border collie,
odd-eyed,
appeared from nowhere
to partake in breakfast—
in our heavy-black-skillet
wild strawberry communion.

Old Backyard Ash

On the metal shelf in the barn there's a piece of scrap wood.
On it is my only poem written since Dad died.

Grief is a blanket
I do not want to share:
I wrap myself up
and into thin air.

I needed to be alone,
always will.
Probably some sort
of rehearsal.

Write a song
(sing to write)
breathe right
so you'll sleep tight.

All trees shedding leaves
except our poplars—custard's last stand:
and they haven't even turned yellow yet!

Steeling myself up
for seeing clearly
wide open
spaces.

What I'm grateful for
now:
the colors that are left
once summer's mask
of chlorophyll is used

and light becomes
our bones:
a flaming white ash
still alive in the Old Backyard.

Pewter and Porcelain

for Shannon

A new book title?
of sight and simplicity
a pattern we can't seem
       to follow
+   +   +   +
Looking at our ceiling fan
move clockwise now,
its lampshade, cream colored
as our kitchen sink (faux-porcelain),
its holding, pewter as the doorknobs we chose
to match Amish ambiance . . .
when suddenly my neighbor's
November 12 text message
coincides with my own internal alarm:
it's time! *H20 for chickens and horses.*
I'm on it (no need to reply).

Rolling home, I feel rich,
guilty with the joys of new treasure:

it's not even breakfast
yet already I have received
emails (read them too), but best of all,
found and fondled
two lovely and warm
free-range Blue Eggs.

First Trip to the Corner Ring

for Kelly

Prudence with age comes,
lolling along the path.

There are so many reasons
for things to go wrong.

The stuff you never noticed
before age-old decrepitude like a vine
began creeping/creeps/has crept in

"on little cat feet"—Carl Sandburg—
like the fog,
the dew on this morning's grass
under newly shod
   feet
as she, my Sister Leto, old, old,
nigh-blind Leopard App mare
carried me past
each wobbly driveway

  up to the ring
at the corner of
VanBuskirk Gulf
and Shaffer.

Together we braved it
all the way there
to meet my friend K.
on *her* shy paint,
a skittish, flighty, thin thing
so well-and-newly-named:
   'Bird.'

Ranch Dance

CC's new cadence: 2-3-4-syllable three-line poems

Expanding Universe

Star tarp
moonlit roof
I dance in song

In the Run-Out

run-in
brutal cold
mare Sister waits

Leopard Appaloosas

patterned
runaways
dream me awake

Groundhog Day Dog

gray dawn
no shadow
except Iris

Cypriot Dream Sunrise

dreams like
a mille-feuille
old suite-mate waves

Rustling Up Words

Take, now, for example,
a new word like 'block chain,'
what does it mean?
I want old words,
words that used to be something,
the hand-held farm tools
tucked behind the grain bin.
My own niche?
Latin teacher, retired.
Romantic agrarian,
turned early out to pasture,
ablative of means
        not
       manner
So maybe I'll settle for local granite
worn slabs swathed in shade
under tall, weeping pines,
small tombstones' upright
staggering, knee-deep in ivy,
time-effaced names,
years and numbered days.

Or maybe I'll just take
whatever rust has not taken,
leave scythe, love and hammer
hanging on the barn wall,
block and chain no longer chafing,
to find, on the web, a new definition,
a sprig of mint green:

"blockchain: old blocks are preserved forever
and new blocks added to the ledger
a special cryptographic key . . .

independent, transparent,
secure, unalterable."

For now I'll chew on this—
before our sacred landscape
becomes just another
writer's block.

Saved by the Pleiades

Tonight's sky is hemorrhaging.

Each star leaves a unique trail.
Long, slow, dawdling,
as if etched in memory,
I feel them all
coming at me.
explode like *Rocks*
that early computer game,
the one we used to play
clustered around the kids
in their almost pitch-dark room.

Today on Star News
a *Perseid shower* was predicted.
But here on our new home's high porch
below a dripping, gutter-less roof
at first I see nothing, but then
I decide to look elsewhere
for seamless stars—

and yes, they arrive!

From near the Pleiades
a plethora comes rushing
into my insomniac, eyes-wide-open range.
I even count them—a record twenty-one!

Alone, barefoot on heat-splintered wood,
neck lolled back, transfixed
beneath an almost-autumn sky,
my nostrils grow cold.
I've lost track of time.

Back inside, upon the kitchen sill
the old wooden egg-timer is lying
on its side, choked with sand.
I turn it upright and watch
it funnel through.

So just what we are:
rock star transformations.

September Heat

You can't eat it,
it melts ice cream from the cone.

The new door of the basement bathroom sticks—
from humidity?

The garden veggies are prolific: they rewrite
the rules, reinventing themselves, still trying to be
indispensable.

How long can we last
without air conditioning?
Call it a heat pump but work its inverse.
Nevertheless, a spade is a spade,
so call it what it is.

Today, pre-dawn, an iridescent horsefly
bit my thigh, exchanged blood for venom
through two layers—leggings and Levis—

to add further complication
to the Climate equation.

Yesterday it was the wet grass and opening
the pasture gate with electric
fence that made me jump.

It's still just September, but (Climate)
change is stuck
in the air.

Shearing

in memoriam Archie Ammons—after reading his "Fasting"
(in Epoch *vol. 52, no. 3)*

Cutting corners, the square becomes
first an octagon, then almost
a circle, compass, sextant.

"This horse needs to be in front
of a plough." Trail riding with dicey
mares behind, two new friends,

changes everything, change is everything:
the gelding knows all this already—
the season's light twice anticipates

hairlessness—a snow-like shedding in grass.
These blades that summer shimmered,
white-bleached, now become like seeds

in someone else's mind: now it's time
for a new batch: thick, lustrous coats,
winterized: for us it's oilskins, raincoats,

extra layers to get us through. Ready, set,
go! How topsy-turvy the Run for the Roses
this year, blown from May to September.

Authentic won by a few strides. Run without a hitch.
Come October, a Preakness filly will beat him by a nose.
You never know. So don't go to great lengths to prepare:

just keep building, extending space to store up (hay)
and once having lost enough to make room for more,
(after all that) just shore up, share the shore.

Sister's Day Off the Ranch

for Laurie

Sunday a.m.
seven-thirty sharp
Laurie's "lorry" arrives.

Not one footfall falters
as the little mare
clambers on,
freshly shod.

Hammond Hill
still at a standstill
as we arrive.

Each cheval with new poop
and Laurie with another notch
in her belt: success
in turning around as needed
in someone's driveway:

the big white rig
with truck black as pitch,
and rough cowboy-leather seats
branded us both for the day
of trail-winding
memories.

So Many Beginnings

So many beginnings, so many Amens.
So many still lives, too many "good friends."
Letters unwritten, and pages torn.
Dreams that are shattered before they are born.

A New Testament is circulating
by mysterious means
in nearly every car.
Every hand holds the recipe, hope,
but gray eyes answer the door.

Your socks are smoking in the oven,
the doctor confuses me with someone
who wears my name, and I explain
I've no middle initial, it's all a mistake.

Someone once told me Humpty Dumpty
was never hard boiled. I've done ate three
this morning, those my mamma gave me,
yet I am bewildered by my own anxiety.

Good gambling throws of the die
the Romans called *Venus.*
To me it's all too much like *snake eyes,*
and no one's winning this time.

Spes (Hope) Is All Around

the Latin word is pronounced // 'space'

When Romans borrowed *Spes*
from the Greeks and freed her
from the darkened box
they knew she was different from the rest,
different from all those woes and diseases
that had peeled out as Pandora peeked in.

Hope alone had stayed, a solitary bright seed,
strong, hard and alive, awaiting human need.

When Hope finally did step out, she was tall,
and her image suddenly sprung up all around,
in Augustan statues, temples, on coins
she was everywhere to be found,
a shining reminder,
right hand extending offertory flower,
left hand lifting billowing skirts
just high enough to reach her stride.

Tartarus Rx

—after President. Biden's Inauguration (2021),
with Amanda Gordon (1st National Youth Poet Laureate)
& upon reading sprung verse by Gerard Manley Hopkins

Skipping lines, slipshod, short *shrift,*
the teeth's *tartar* is quick to accumulate—
especially when your brushing's been bad.
Don't wait for a dentist to fix it.
You can count on *calculus* to be there—
those plural little stones ensnaring
the gum line, coating inscapes
of dreams like dry-mouth moths,
fluttering like faded prayer flags
tattered in neglect . . .

just as woods fills in pasture,
beginning with the mossing over of brook stone,
and then a march of thistles and thorns,
next, nettles, and high anthills only
pangolins or possums might dream of.
Beneath briars circling serpentine,
bursts of burrs linger to latch on.

Not only that! Tall tamaracks and wily scotch pines
have made their seed march
from our clumped, old neighboring graveyard
so peopled with past all its steeples are broken,
(though dutifully mown and now and then
renewed with miniature flags)
among the worn-out epitaphs.
until all that's left to read is this,
between the crooked teeth
of too-old tombstones,

just read between the lines: *Don't forget*
to cradle life. It's not enough to simply
'Keep your nose clean!' (a savvy Navy saying
Dad often used).

And when it comes to teeth,
as with any regime,
be vigilant, brush often, with a light, circular motion.

A simple mix of baking soda and salt is all you need
to keep tartar at bay,
both clean and short,
like good prose,
or even, occasionally, a poem

that comes straight back from Tartarus.

Temporary Illiteracy

for Judy S.

Dolor infandum
can cause it too

it's hard to know
when it will hit you

illiteracy" means no reading or writing
"temporary" means no long-term sighting

the signs are everywhere
hermeneutic

so close them now!
tablet, app, book eye and lid

inside wordless prayer
images are dancing

to help you out
of the dark cave

where you can only feel the light
no fire, no gathering, no wall shadows

just white light coming from within:
a lone butterfly's migration, all pleasure

away from words and captions:
sleep on it, stay within the *id.*

Two September Haiku

for Mom—Florence Adams Clark (poet), 2018

Hurricane Florence
testing our green metal roof
taps out two-inch rain

three blue spots missing
Black Swallowtail sails her last
across tangled grass

Untact

These were once
my *keywords:*
dactylic hexameter
epic poetry
Homeric heroes
word cadences
lost pitch of song

And my precious digs?
Nausikaa, a princess
washing, singing
the river clean:
laughter matrilineal.

Now far gone are
those shining epithets,
patronymics too,
replaced by machines.
Today, editing, I find a new word
freshly flagged:
      untact (stet).

Coined in South Korea,
it evokes 'intact'—
a dream economy where
distance-workers, Covid-free,
keep pace with automation:
no touch, no share,
not breath, not smell, nor taste.
You can work from anywhere.

But as dirty laundry, plastics,
acronyms, all keep piling up
in swirling islands somewhere in the Pacific,

there's a vision of a new world
with more and more AI—artificial intelligence—
—ai, ai, ai,—how quickly we mourn loss.
Who will take in clothes and shrouds, fresh, sun-dried?
Estuaries, will they ever again be clean?
Who will greet the heroes coming home?
And Nausikaa? Who knew her name
meant all along: "the burner of ships"?

Take Time to Breathe

for Geoff—Valentine's Day 2020

Take time to breathe,
listen to the heart—
yours, and his—so close,
accessible.

Shape waxen earplugs,
block out all snoring—
his—and yours—
both love's labor.

Keep hands warm,
hold lightening tight,
winter moon rinsing
molten dreams.

Love is a letter,
time a weird mask,
stars dot the horizon,
shape a new path.

So my V (Valentine),
help smile, breathe right,
tuck me in, to your heart,
for a while tonight.

Waiting for ACL Surgery

winter of 2017—and thanks to our neighbor Ed G.,
this poem is now a song for guitar

Think sloth,
think snake,
make no mistake.

Move slow,
write fast,
treasure the past.

Keep strong
your song
in the predawn.

Our old snow's fresh
Concolor Christmas tree
still smells of oranges.

Each needle
Innumerable,
mute, immovable.

For now I'm under
House Arrest: wearing
a knee bracelet.

P.S. Boo hoo! Tant pis!

Bury my heart at Broken Knee.

Was Herod paranoid?

after Masada, 1977

Frozen bison
bones on dunes of sand.
Two hawks sailing.
Wind a westerly shadow.
When we begin our descent
down Snake Path,
goats cross our way,
and each day is wedged
between edges of sand
beaten into cornice.

It's late November,
in Ithaca and Cornell again,
a two-years old image
shimmers on mother's sheets:
it's a family reunion slide show (!)
and the dunes are upside down.

Oedipus Wrecks softball recruits
get ready to bat.
A tragedy of new vision
winters in the Temple Zeus.

Your eyes, grandfather,
so keenly obstinate,
gather me into other worlds,
echo me an answer
I can almost reach:

I am old beyond my time
because I refuse to accept
my time, my time.

OBLIQUE
(Old Blues: Love Is Quite Un-Equal)

(i)

Something's gone
A-
stray
like a Jacob's ladder
but going nowhere
(fast).

Pinioned to adversity,
this rock,
Promethean,
entangles me—
till I spill
my guts out.

Every time
something doesn't
work out
I go running
and (then) it doesn't
seem to matter
so much:

a deer with three legs
survives (maybe)
in the copse,
briar thicket
of a gully
on the power line.

(ii)

Fragments from February:

Feb 2

- "Weep the boweevil"
    -popped into my head during a faculty meeting

- "Woe, the bow evil"

- "Woo"
    -found a blue heart on the ground
    -black ice tonight

Feb 3

Holding on
to life on hold

(iii)

Years after dispelling Eros,
I finally learn to spell
the word "boll"
(like "bowl" not "beau").
Google it: a cotton-eating bug
found in folksong,
politics, history and science.

I surmise it just so happens
that the Upside-Down
Rule of Appearances
versus the True Nature of Things
holds true in Texas (!) after all—

new research has shown
that "*weeping lovegrass*
can serve
as an overwintering
habitat
for the *boll weevil*."

So weep away.

But don't for a moment think
there's nobody watching.

(iv)

An old god,
Eros must have mixed up
his magic: this arrow
isn't working
the way it should:
my heart is still
glowing with affection—
for everyone—
and sometimes
I even focus long enough
to forget.
But the older goddess,
Nature, is always there
when you need her:

walking home by streetlight,
rain has made the trees droop,
my forehead touches
the tip of the finger
of a wet maple leaf,
and I thank her for this blessing

on the bright side of the road.

Winter Catharsis

Time repeating itself,
the season's starting over:
El Nino, global warming,
mixed it up.

In the dell of the pasture
sunrise white-gold-platinum,
clouds and blue patches, illuminate:
the old apple tree's centennial.

I'm still picking apples up,
plus "apples by the road"
and filling in hoofprints
with frozen piles of pie.

Winter's resin: the truth comes out,
no whitewashing snow,
just a smattering of days and days
of untouched dog poop, thawed out.

So I shovel it too,
to a makeshift graveyard
well past the manure pile,
past the base of a tall white pine,

above the bracket of thorns
that is our forest slope
to the gulf below. Turning back
up to the house after the satisfaction of chores,

I find our green metal roof, so steep, is still
tinged silver with frost, but seen from back inside,
its tears are dripping, golden from a silver fern,
winter's catharsis, as ashes from an urn.

The River

somewhere near Athens, Georgia, 1985

A river following forever
said to me one day,
"Why do you never see me?
When will you go away?"
To him I dipped my hat
and swallowed my offense,
"It's because I run beside you,
where the thicket's dense."
But seeing how I'd caught my breath
as well as 'suaged my thirst
he carried on with laughter,
his mischief deep as mirth.
And as I stood there tongue-tied
I glimpsed his tawny hide—
t'was gold and silver-chased like sun—
I watched the river glide.

Two Shooting Stars

for Audrey

June 2019

Two shooting stars tonight—again!
One tailed like a comet,
the other too, but smaller,
shooting horizontal
north to south
In the eastern sky,
where only yesterday
the moon rose
at second night
while I gulped in the cold
from our window,
airing my lungs out,
peering into the dark pasture
to follow the white mare's
every move
in a sky lit by the undersurface,
rising
among a sky of
mare's tails.

Homeostasis

Today your letter arrived with old news,
the first good I've known for so long.
It's bad times, you say, are hanging on
in Bodega Bay, where the fish still rattle
on the beach made of grits instead of sand
'cause you're so hungry even early morning salt
ain't enough to satiate your stasis.

Telling stories to empty hands at night,
sometimes you strike it rich:
a deep green vein hidden in your wrist
is still wriggling. Turning blue in the morning,
you find your place among friends.

But as the sun clambers
over to your side,
blood runs red,
and the nail or thumb you're hitting
for a dollar an hour just won't do
what the tomatoes are doing here:

the west coast is turning green
while the winter gathers me
and you are still
watching the shore,
birds.

Dead Bells of Ireland

Dead Bells of Ireland cannot
hold a candle to this lady's cap:
their centerpiece,
she dances fore and center,
a celebrity
ushering in
the opened coffins'
ivory bones
with such lovely gesture
to her left.

"De Brevitate Vitae"
oh how the drinking boys
for centuries would sing:

Gaudeamus igitur,

Iuvenes dum sumus,

Gaudeamus igitur,

Iuvenes dum sumus,

Post jucundam juventutem,

Post molestam senectutem,

Nos habebit humus,

Nos habebit humus.

Their fifth stanza, so apt, like these

Vivant omnes virgines

Faciles, formosae

Vivant et mulieres

Bonae, laboriosae.

Long live all girls,

Easy [and] beautiful!

Long live [mature] women too,

Tender, lovable,

Good, [and] hard-working.

These are five women, 'witches,' dancing!
Whose prima ballerina has feet foreshadowing
a life just like their own: feet are
all the same, wide, bare and mud-splashed
yet still they fly across the floor.

Parodied cliches, yet admired:
shoulders, forearms storied
muscles from a lifetime
of field labor and chores.
Determined to have fun:
their chins jut out,
and one's upturned nose
is longer than Pinochio's.

On the dancer's right, in a dark
but profiled foreground,
an old woman is plunked down,
her cane held upward
as if in half-salute,
she gazes up, mesmerized, bewitched
by the short chiffon-dressed maiden
in whom (perhaps) she sees her own
lost youth flown fleeting past,
and beneath the curled white fronds
of her own soddy old bonnet
therein may lie a self-portrait
of our anonymous
Scottish (?)
artist.

Old Roman Poem: Above the Gianicolo[*]

Rome, 1978

The people chosen know themselves to be clay,
some days even dust.
Who's there to trust? I know no names,
Death nor AfterDeath nor AfterLife as some would say.
Only that the Oak might know,
And I, as a leaf, blown far afield across the burning pyre,
higher than sense or sight,
might be
somewhere beyond the moon,
seeing naught of its bright face,
but only the cold, the bright invisible,
invincible darkness, blind
even to myself.

---

* This poem was written near the same fountain & park where Bob Dylan used to hang out—as witnessed in his song 'Isis'—among others.

God Puzzle and a Reckless Zephyr

I am everywhere You are not
yet
You are everywhere I am.

As poet, I am here to record
this thistledown wind.
I am its curator.
With poison pen
or golf pencil stub
on birchbark skin
I try to keep track
of its comings and goings,
arrivals, vanishing, reappearances.

Feckless Zephyr, spring wind too strong,
you are relentless in doubling our trouble,
creaking staccato enclaves,
sowing the air with spheres
of spikey pink stubble—
Corona-shaped pollen.

Yet every now and then,
off you go, thither and yon,
suddenly softer,
lisping whispers
drawing us out with your song:

"Spring is here, why not
take up residence,
breathe deeply in,
exhale fear."

Wintergarden Cold War *Redux*

for Armando

Sixty some years ago
how could we know
that planting a seed
depletes soil,
supplements detritus?

How could we know
democracies would clash,
disperse tendrils
and fail, nations splinter,
leave behind a trail
of broken promises?

How could we know
ergo or *Q.E.D.,*
Time's vassal, is
quod erat demonstrandum
('stated to signify the Author's
overall argument
has just been proven')?

No system remains intact.
Testimonials from those
who were there are gone,
too soon or too late,
recycled Cassandra-like moments,
predicting the future from forgotten
rotting roots, tubers . . .
Must we keep having to stumble
over them, must we?

Yes, we must now, yes,
in this cruel spring,
find the passion
and time to tell
our stories,
to listen to one another,
to care enough to learn.
We must outlive and leave behind
the Wintergarden, allow ourselves
to be unburdened,
hearts lighter, and face a gentler reason:
we must need find compassion,
instill empathy, reseed.

Judy Collins Concert (Homer, NY) 2022

In Homer, in an old Baptist church converted to Performing Arts
Judy's own new songs enshrine moments from native Colorado.
Later, I learn that her father, Homer, a talented, blind radio DJ,
moved the family from Seattle to Denver in 1949.
She was ten. As she said, he promised her Paris . . . and a dance.
It wouldn't be her last. Her black sequined shirt reflecting
diamonds,
shimmering rainbows, at 83, she educates us.
Gone her canonical long-flowing hair, now newly shorn,
her Joan Baez' style post-Covid haircut assures
that face hides nothing, holds only bold, strong lines.
She is angular, rangy and strong, as her voice.
Between her story-songs, she talks in-between,
sharing one piece of news that shocked me thoroughly:
what she'd discovered about Thomas Merton, yes, the same
contemplative poet my own Colorado Mom adored.
Bullet holes were recently found in his exhumed body
—it turns out that he was shot—at the Thai monastery.
No hapless victim of electric shock stepping out of the shower, no,
that was part of the coverup. And now, Judy says, there's this
new book, telling it as it is, and was: Merton's model for peace
during the Viet Nam war
had become so popular . . . it had earned him some
enemies, and no longer cherished under the auspices
of the Catholic Church, though mutually distanced, he was
buried without truth, only injustice, to sleep with this lie, carefully
shrouded,
while time, unblinking, turned a blind eye.

Wishbone Trails

March 20, 2022

Angel foot deer trails,
bone skinned,
dot the highway.
DOT tangerine lights
spooking cars from afar
pick up bodies
in the back of pickups.

This morning's fog
thicker than the oatmeal
that sticks inside me
alongside a free-range egg.

I'm coming in
to work outside.

Crossing the Tompkins-Cortland
county line
NPR Amy Goodman's show
gets scrambled into Christian Rock
and blasts me past Virgil, NY

but not before
these subtitles
rise from within me:
(we must)
*Say Yes
to the No
'No Fly Zone'*—

Ukraine, we are closer than you think.

A first ever IFM QWERTY poem

Today my first request is this:
a lady who listens to the keys,
pauses, circles back, asks kindly
for words as on a breeze: a bird
whose wings dip and turn,
a silhouette, my swallow, catching
a poem in the morning, the new day
that shines shyly forward,
the first customer of my new
abode.

May your days stay long

If you are sleeping now, Mama,
that is good,
for the heat of August is strong
and days long...

But dream of me by the dock
in a pocket of shade
where together we have wandered
and played at song...

on a 1926 Typewriter whose name
means 'Crown' and like a baby's
head, remains soft as a fontenelle
while words emerge...

from you, from Dad (musica), from me

About the Author

Carolyn Clark, Ph.D. Classics (Latin and Ancient Greek), was born and raised in Ithaca, NY, and worked as a teacher in Montgomery County Public Schools, Maryland before moving back to the Finger Lakes region seven years ago. An experienced writing coach and editor, the author now also enjoys creating "made for you" poems at the Ithaca Farmers Market on her family's 1926 Smith-Corona typewriter (aka QWERTY). She also adores horses, writing woodlands lyric poetry, and finding mythology everywhere.

Made in the USA
Middletown, DE
15 June 2023

32665496R00056